Quilt

Fons&Porter

Modern Baby Quilts

FROM MARIANNE & LIZ

We're thrilled to bring you this collection of some of our very favorite baby quilts. The projects we've included are among our most popular of all time. You'll find patchwork for all skill levels, plus bits of darling appliqué. Enjoy the beautiful photography as you browse through the pages to find a quilt that's just right for you and the baby you love. You'll also appreciate our trademarked *Sew Easy* lessons that will guide you via step-by-step photography through any project-specific special techniques. Have fun stitching these baby quilts!

HAPPY QUILTING,

Marianne + Liz

FONS & PORTER STAFF
Editors-in-Chief Marianne Fons and Liz Porter

Editor Jean Nolte
Managing Editor Debra Finan
Associate Editor Diane Tomlinson
Technical Writer Kristine Peterson

Art Director Kelsey Allan

Interactive Editor Sheyenne Manning
Sewing Specialist Colleen Tauke
Contributing Photographers Dean Tanner, Kathryn Gamble
Contributing Photo Assistant Mary Mouw

Publisher Kristi Loeffelholz
Advertising Managers Cristy Adamski, Lisa O'Bryan
Retail Manager Sharon Hart
Web Site Manager Phillip Zacharias
IT Manager Denise Donnarumma
Fons & Porter Staff Shelle Goodwin, Anne Welker, Karla Wesselmann, Tony Jacobson

F+W, A CONTENT + ECOMMERCE COMPANY
Chairman and CEO David Nussbaum
CFO & COO James Ogle
President Sara Domville
President David Blansfield
Chief Digital Officer Chad Phelps
Vice President/ E-Commerce Lucas Hilbert
Senior Vice President/Operations Phil Graham
Vice President/ E-Commerce Stacie Berger

Our Mission Statement
Our goal is for you to enjoy making quilts as much as we do.

LEISURE ARTS STAFF
Vice President of Editorial Susan White Sullivan
Creative Art Director Katherine Laughlin
Publications Director Leah Lampirez
Special Projects Director Susan Frantz Wiles
Prepress Technician Stephanie Johnson

President and Chief Executive Officer Fred F. Pruss
Senior Vice President of Operations Jim Dittrich
Vice President of Sales-Retail Books Martha Adams
Vice President of Mass Market Bob Bewighouse
Vice President of Technology and Planning Laticia Mull Dittrich
Controller Tiffany P. Childers
Information Technology Director Brian Roden
Director of E-Commerce Mark Hawkins
Manager of E-Commerce Robert Young
Retail Customer Service Manager Stan Raynor

Library of Congress Control Number: 2014944701
ISBN-13/EAN: 978-1-4647-1604-1
UPC: 0-28906-06363-9

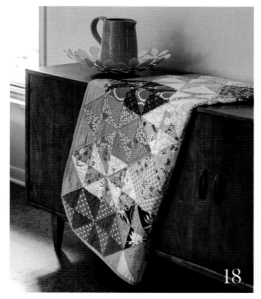  

PROJECTS

LEARN

Finished size: 48" × 48"
Quilt by Angela Brichacek.

LI'L ROCK STAR

A weekend project, a baby quilt, something to toss over the piano...Think of this quilt as a little black dress—a versatile addition to any collection.

CUTTING

Measurements include ¼" seam allowances. Border strips are exact length needed. You may want to cut them longer to allow for piecing variations.

FROM RED PRINT, CUT:
- 3 (4⅞"-wide) strips. From strips, cut 18 (4⅞") squares. Cut squares in half diagonally to make 36 half-square triangles.

FROM GREEN PRINT, CUT:
- 3 (4⅞"-wide) strips. From strips, cut 18 (4⅞") squares. Cut squares in half diagonally to make 36 half-square triangles.

FROM BLUE PRINT, CUT:
- 4 (2½"-wide) strips. From strips, cut 2 (2½" × 28½") top and bottom inner borders and 2 (2½" × 24½") side inner borders.

FROM BLACK PRINT, CUT:
- 4 (2½"-wide) strips for strip sets.

FROM WHITE PRINT, CUT:
- 4 (2½"-wide) strips for strip sets.

FROM YELLOW PRINT, CUT:
- 5 (6½"-wide) strips. From 2 strips, cut 2 (6½" × 36½") side outer borders. Piece remaining strips to make 2 (6½" × 48½") top and bottom outer borders.
- 6 (2¼"-wide) strips for binding.

Materials

½ yard red print

½ yard green print

⅜ yard blue print

⅜ yard black print

⅜ yard white print

1½ yards yellow print

3 yards backing fabric

Twin-size quilt batting

CENTER ASSEMBLY

1. Join 1 red print half-square triangle and 1 green print half-square triangle as shown in *Triangle-Square Diagrams*. Make 36 triangle-squares.

2. Lay out triangle-squares as shown in *Quilt Top Assembly Diagram*. Join into horizontal rows; join rows to complete quilt center.

QUILT ASSEMBLY

1. Add blue print side inner borders to quilt center. Add blue print top and bottom inner borders to quilt.

2. Join 1 black print strip and 1 white print strip as shown in *Strip Set Diagram*. Make 4 strip sets. From strip sets, cut 64 (2½"-wide) segments.

3. Referring to *Quilt Top Assembly Diagram*, join 14 segments to make 1 side middle border. Make 2 side middle borders. In the same manner, join 18 segments to make top middle border. Repeat for bottom middle border.

4. Add side middle borders to quilt center. Add top and bottom middle borders to quilt.

5. Repeat for yellow print outer borders.

FINISHING

1. Divide backing into 2 (1½-yard) lengths. Cut 1 piece in half lengthwise to make 2 narrow panels. Join 1 narrow panel to wider panel. Remaining panel is extra and can be used to make a hanging sleeve.

2. Layer backing, batting, and quilt top; baste. Quilt as desired. Quilt shown was quilted with an allover design of loops and stars (*Quilting Diagram*).

3. Join 2¼"-wide yellow print strips into 1 continuous piece for straight-grain French-fold binding. Add binding to quilt. ✛

Triangle-Square Diagrams

2½"

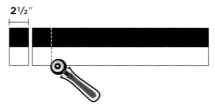

Strip Set Diagram

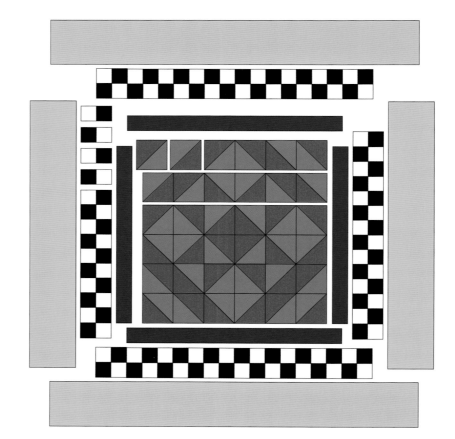

Quilt Top Assembly Diagram

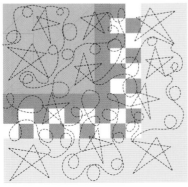

Quilting Diagram

Angela Brichacek sews or quilts something every day. She is a longarm quilter who loves watching quilting on TV and reading about it in magazines and on the internet.

Finished size: 46" × 46"

Quilt by Kristi Loeffelholz.
Quilted by Kelly Van Vliet.

Boo's Nursery

Who's got the cutest baby room on the block? You do.

CUTTING

Measurements include ¼" seam allowances.

FROM GRAY SOLID, CUT:
- 8 (3½"-wide) strips. From strips, cut 4 (3½" × 23½") H rectangles and 4 (3½" × 20½") G rectangles.
- 5 (2½"-wide) strips for binding.

FROM ORANGE PRINT FAT QUARTER, CUT:
- 2 (5½"-wide) strips. From strips, cut 4 (5½") A squares.

FROM GREEN PRINT FAT QUARTER, CUT:
- 4 (3½"-wide) strips. From strips, cut 4 (3½" × 8½") C rectangles and 4 (3½" × 5½") B rectangles.

FROM BLUE PRINT FAT QUARTER, CUT:
- 4 (3½"-wide) strips. From strips, cut 4 (3½" × 11½") D rectangles and 4 (3½" × 8½") C rectangles.

FROM ORANGE PRINT ½ YARD PIECE, CUT:
- 4 (3½"-wide) strips. From strips, cut 4 (3½" × 14½") E rectangles and 4 (3½" × 11½") D rectangles.

FROM YELLOW PRINT ½ YARD PIECE, CUT:
- 4 (3½"-wide) strips. From strips, cut 4 (3½" × 17½") F rectangles and 4 (3½" × 14½") E rectangles.

FROM BLUE PRINT ½ YARD PIECE, CUT:
- 4 (3½"-wide) strips. From strips, cut 4 (3½" × 20½") G rectangles and 4 (3½" × 17½") F rectangles.

Materials

1¼ yards gray solid

1 fat quarter* orange print

1 fat quarter* green print

1 fat quarter* blue print

½ yard each of 3 assorted prints (orange, blue, and yellow)

1⅜ yards 60"-wide plush fabric for backing

Twin-size quilt batting

*Fat quarter = 18" × 20"

BLOCK ASSEMBLY

1. Lay out 1 A square and 1 set of B–H rectangles as shown in *Block Assembly Diagrams*.

2. Add rectangles to A square in alphabetical order to complete 1 block (*Block Diagram*).

3. Make 4 blocks.

QUILT ASSEMBLY

1. Lay out blocks as shown in *Quilt Top Assembly Diagram*.

2. Join blocks into rows; join rows to complete quilt top.

FINISHING

1. Layer backing, batting, and quilt top; baste. Quilt as desired. Quilt shown was quilted in the ditch and with zigzag and straight line designs in blocks (*Quilting Diagram*).

2. Join 2½"-wide gray strips into 1 continuous piece for straight-grain French-fold binding. Add binding to quilt.

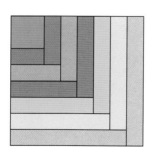

Block Assembly Diagrams

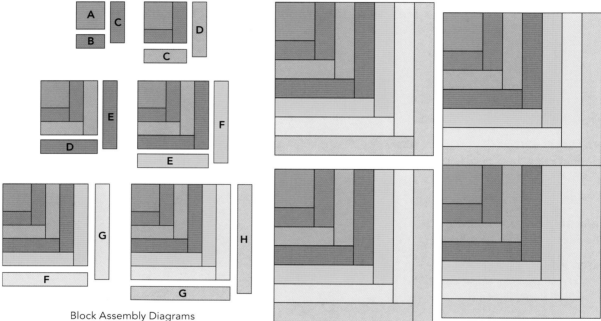

Quilt Top Assembly Diagram

Block Diagram

Quilting Diagram

Curtains

by Shantelle Hope

MATERIALS

5 yards gray chevron print

CUTTING

FROM GRAY CHEVRON PRINT, CUT:
- 2 (26" × 89") panels.

CURTAIN ASSEMBLY

1. Along sides and bottom of each panel, press under ½", then ½". To hem sides and bottom of each panel, stitch close to first fold.

2. Press under ½", then 3" at top of each panel. Stitch close to first fold to make casing for rod. ✦

Changing Pad Cover

by Shantelle Hope

MATERIALS

1 yard 60"-wide plush fabric
1 yard ³⁄₈"-wide elastic

CUTTING

FROM PLUSH FABRIC, CUT:
- 1 (32" × 48") rectangle.

CHANGING PAD ASSEMBLY

1. Referring to *Changing Pad Diagram*, cut 8" square from each corner of plush rectangle.

2. Referring to *Corner Stitching Diagrams*, pin sides A and B together, right sides facing. Stitch with ½" seam. Repeat for remaining corners.

3. Press under ½" on raw edges of changing pad. Press under 1" to form casing. Stitch close to first fold, leaving 1" opening to make casing for elastic.

4. Insert elastic in casing. Secure ends of elastic. Whipstitch opening closed. ✦

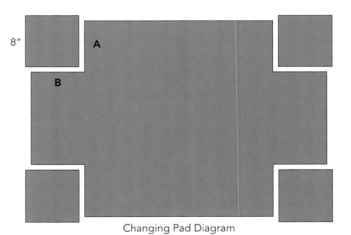

Changing Pad Diagram

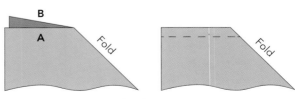

Corner Stitching Diagrams

Crib Sheet

Designed by Fons & Porter Staff | Made by Shantelle Hope

MATERIALS

2 yards gray solid

1½ yards (¼"-wide) elastic

CUTTING

FROM GRAY SOLID, CUT:
- 1 (42" × 67") rectangle.

CRIB SHEET ASSEMBLY

1. Referring to *Crib Sheet Diagram*, cut a 7" square from each corner of gray rectangle. Mark a dot 12½" from corner on long edge of sheet. Mark another dot ½" from first dot. Repeat for remaining corners.

2. Referring to *Corner Stitching Diagrams*, pin sides A and B together, right sides facing. Stitch with ½" seam. Repeat for remaining corners.

3. Press under ¼" on raw edges of sheet. Press under ½" to form casing. Stitch close to first fold, leaving ½" openings between dots to insert elastic.

4. From elastic, cut 2 (27"-long) pieces. Insert 1 piece of elastic in casing and thread through short end of sheet. Secure ends of elastic at dots. Repeat for opposite end of sheet. Stitch openings closed.

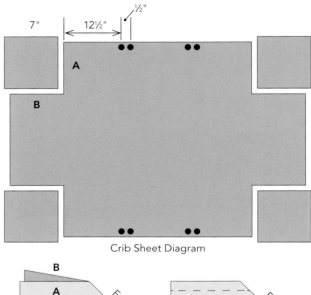

Crib Sheet Diagram

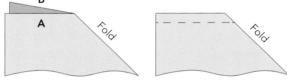

Corner Stitching Diagrams

Pillow

by Shantelle Hope
15" × 15"

MATERIALS

½ yard gray print

16" square pillow insert

CUTTING

Measurements include ¼" seam allowances.

FROM GRAY PRINT, CUT:
- 1 (15½"-wide) strip. From strip, cut 1 (15½") square for front and 2 (15½" × 10½") rectangles for back.

PILLOW ASSEMBLY

1. Hem 1 (15½") edge of each backing rectangle.

2. Overlap hemmed edges of backing rectangles, making square the same size as front. Baste overlapped edges together (*Backing Diagram*).

3. Place front square atop backing, right sides facing. Stitch around outer edges. Clip corners. Turn right side out.

4. Insert pillow form through opening in back.

Backing Diagram

Crib Skirt

by Shantelle Hope
28" × 52"

MATERIALS

2¼ yards blue print

1 yard green print

1½ yards muslin for base

CUTTING

FROM BLUE PRINT, CUT:
- 6 (12½"-wide) strips. From strips, cut 6 (12½" × 30") A rectangles.

FROM GREEN PRINT, CUT:
- 6 (4½"-wide) strips. From strips, cut 6 (4½" × 30") B rectangles.

FROM MUSLIN, CUT:
- 1 (53" × 29") rectangle.

CRIB SKIRT ASSEMBLY

1. Join 1 blue print A rectangle and 1 green print B rectangle to make 1 panel as shown in *Crib Skirt Assembly Diagrams.*

2. Press under ½", then ½" along sides and bottom of panel. Stitch close to first fold to hem sides and bottom of panel.

3. Make 6 panels.

4. With right sides facing, join muslin rectangle and panels as shown, using a ½" seam allowance. Panels on long sides of muslin will overlap in center. +

Kristi Loeffelholz has worked in the craft and quilt publishing industry for more than a decade. She designed the quilt for her sister's baby shower gift and appreciates all the help she received from the Fons & Porter staff.

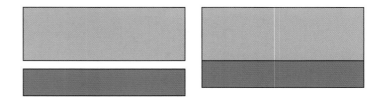

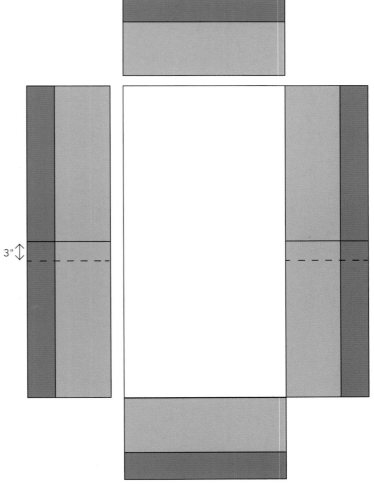

3"

Crib Skirt Assembly Diagrams

Finished size: 38½" × 39½"
Quilt designed by Vanessa Christenson.
Made by Lissa Alexander.

Baby Life Quilt

The words on this quilt are quality directions for life. Easy appliqué and a modern palette elevate this brilliant baby quilt. Quilt in baby's birthday, weight, and name to up the heirloom factor.

Materials

- 1⅜ yards yellow plaid for background and outer border
- ½ yard orange solid for letters and binding
- 4 fat eighths* solid fabrics in green, blue, and brown for letters
- 4 fat eighths* assorted prints in green, blue, and brown for inner border
- Paper-backed fusible web
- 1¼ yards backing fabric
- Crib-size quilt batting

*fat eighth = 9" × 20"

CUTTING

Measurements include ¼" seam allowances. Border strips are exact length needed. (You may want to cut them longer to allow for piecing variations, though.) Patterns for letters are on page 17. Follow manufacturer's instructions for using fusible web.

FROM YELLOW PLAID, CUT:
- 1 (34" × 35") background rectangle.
- 4 (2"-wide) strips. From strips, cut 2 (2" × 39") top and bottom outer borders and 2 (2" × 37") side outer borders.

FROM ORANGE SOLID, CUT:
- 5 (2½"-wide) strips for binding.
- 1 each e, a, t, and period.

FROM GREEN SOLID, CUT:
- 1 each p, l, a, y, and period.

FROM BLUE SOLID, CUT:
- 1 each s, l, p, and period.
- 2 e.

FROM BROWN SOLID, CUT:
- 1 each r, p, a, t, and period.
- 2 e.

FROM ASSORTED PRINTS, CUT A TOTAL OF:
- 10 (1½"-wide) strips. Cut strips into various lengths from 3" to 10".

APPLIQUÉ

1. Referring to photo on page 16, position letters and periods on background rectangle.

2. Fuse in place. If desired, machine appliqué letters using matching thread and blanket or zigzag stitch.

QUILT ASSEMBLY

1. Referring to *Quilt Top Assembly Diagram* on page 16, join assorted print strips to make 1 (35"-long) side inner border. Make 2 side inner borders. Add borders to quilt center.

2. In the same manner, make 2 (36"-long) top and bottom inner borders. Add borders to quilt.

3. Add side outer borders to quilt center; add top and bottom outer borders to quilt.

Sew Smart

It's best to stitch around letters if quilt will be used and washed.

FINISHING

1. Layer backing, batting, and quilt top; baste. Quilt as desired. Quilt shown was quilted with an allover design (*Quilting Diagram*).

2. Join 2½"-wide orange strips into 1 continuous piece for straight-grain French-fold binding. Add binding to quilt. ✛

Quilting Diagram

Quilt Top Assembly Diagram

Vanessa Christenson is a quilter, designer, blogger, author, and mom based in Iowa. Her first book, *Make It Sew Modern*, was published by Martingale & Company.

Patterns are shown full size and are reversed for use with fusible web. Add $\frac{3}{16}''$ seam allowance for hand appliqué.

Finished size: 40" × 48"

Quilt by Faith Jones.

Candy Pinwheels

Take a handful of free-wheeling half-square triangles out for a spin! If the colder weather's got you down, we suggest candy.

Materials

NOTE: This quilt is backed with soft, short pile plush fabric.

- 36 fat quarters* assorted prints in orange, red, gold, blue, pink, gray, and green
- 1 yard turquoise solid for quilt and binding
- 1½ yards 60"-wide plush fabric for backing
- Crib-size quilt batting

*fat quarter = 18" × 20"

CUTTING

Measurements include ¼" seam allowances.

FROM EACH FAT QUARTER, CUT:

- 1 (4⅞"-wide) strip. From strip, cut 3 (4⅞") squares. Cut squares in half diagonally to make 6 half-square triangles.

FROM TURQUOISE SOLID, CUT:

- 2 (4⅞"-wide) strips. From strips, cut 10 (4⅞") squares. Cut squares in half diagonally to make 20 half-square triangles.
- 6 (2½"-wide) strips for binding.

PINWHEEL BLOCK ASSEMBLY

1. Join 2 half-square print triangles as shown in *Triangle-Square Diagrams*. Make 17 sets of 4 matching triangle-squares.

2. Lay out 1 set of triangle-squares as shown in *Block Assembly Diagram*. Join into rows; join rows to complete 1 block (*Block Diagram*). Make 17 blocks.

Triangle-Square Diagrams

Block Assembly Diagram

Block Diagram

Block Row Diagrams

QUILT ASSEMBLY

1. Lay out blocks referring to the photo on page 21 and *Block Row Diagrams* on page 19. Join 6 blocks to make 1 Block Row. Make 2 Block Rows. Join 5 blocks to make 1 partial Center Block Row.

2. Lay out block rows and half-square triangles as shown in *Quilt Top Assembly Diagram*, matching half-square triangles with colors in adjacent blocks.

3. Join individual half-square triangles to make triangle-squares.

4. Join triangle-squares and remaining individual half-square triangles into vertical rows.

5. Join rows to complete quilt top.

FINISHING

1. Layer backing, batting, and quilt top; baste. Quilt as desired. Quilt shown was outline quilted around triangle-squares (*Quilting Diagram*).

2. Join 2½"-wide turquoise strips into 1 continuous piece for straight-grain French-fold binding. Add binding to quilt. ✦

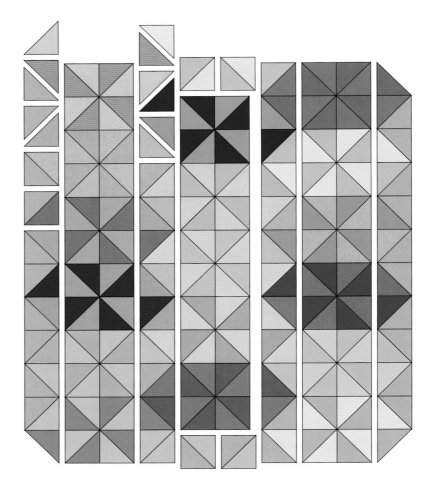

Quilt Top Assembly Diagram

Quilting Diagram

Faith Jones has explored all aspects of quilting—from fabric design to pattern creation. She is an active member of the online modern quilting community and enjoys sharing tutorials and quiltalongs on her blog.

Finished size: 45" × 63"
Finished block size: 6 (18") blocks

Quilt designed by Jodie Davis.
Made by Heidi Kalmakoff.

Hush Little Baby

Make this quilt in gentle tones of purple and blue to wrap around your little one.

CUTTING

Measurements include ¼" seam allowances. Border strips are exact length needed. You may want to make them longer to allow for piecing variations.

To cut triangles for triangle-squares using the Fons & Porter Half & Quarter Ruler, download *Sew Easy: Cutting Half-Square Triangles* at *FonsandPorter.com/CHST*. If you are not using the Fons & Porter Half & Quarter Ruler, use the cutting note instructions given below.

FROM CREAM PRINT #1 FAT QUARTER, CUT:
- 3 (6½"-wide) strips. From strips, cut 6 (6½") A squares.

FROM REMAINING CREAM PRINT FAT QUARTERS, CUT A TOTAL OF:
- 5 (6½"-wide) strips. From strips, cut 24 (6½" × 3½") C rectangles.
- 24 (3½") B squares.

FROM ASSORTED PURPLE PRINT FAT QUARTERS, CUT A TOTAL OF:
- 6 (3½"-wide) strips. From strips, cut 48 half-square D triangles.
  NOTE: If NOT using the Fons & Porter Half & Quarter Ruler to cut the D triangles, cut 6 (3⅞"-wide) strips. From strips, cut 24 (3⅞") squares. Cut squares in half diagonally to make 48 half-square D triangles.

FROM ASSORTED BLUE PRINT FAT QUARTERS, CUT A TOTAL OF:
- 6 (3½"-wide) strips. From strips, cut 48 half-square D triangles.
  NOTE: If NOT using the Fons & Porter Half & Quarter Ruler to cut the D triangles, cut 6 (3⅞"-wide) strips. From strips, cut 24 (3⅞") squares. Cut squares in half diagonally to make 48 half-square D triangles.
- 14 (3½"-wide) strips. From strips, cut 68 (3½") B squares.
- 12 (2¼"-wide) strips for binding.

FROM TAN PRINT #1 FAT QUARTER, CUT:
- 5 (3½"-wide) strips. From strips, cut 24 (3½") B squares.

FROM TAN PRINT, CUT:
- 5 (2"-wide) strips. From 2 strips, cut 2 (2" × 39½") top and bottom inner borders. Piece remaining strips to make 2 (2" × 54½") side inner borders.

FROM REMAINING TAN PRINT FAT QUARTERS, CUT A TOTAL OF:
- 12 (3½"-wide) strips. From strips, cut 96 half-square D triangles.
  NOTE: If NOT using the Fons & Porter Half & Quarter Ruler to cut the D triangles, cut 5 (3⅞"-wide) strips. From strips, cut 48 (3⅞") squares. Cut squares in half diagonally to make 96 half-square D triangles.

BLOCK ASSEMBLY

1. Join 1 tan print D triangle and 1 blue print D triangle as shown in *Triangle-Square Diagrams*. Make 48 blue triangle-squares.

2. In the same manner, make 48 purple triangle-squares using tan print and purple print D triangles.

3. Lay out 4 tan print #1 B squares, 4 cream print B squares, 4 cream print C rectangles, 8 blue triangle-squares, 8 purple triangle-squares, and 1 cream print #1 A square as shown in *Block Assembly Diagram*. Join into rows; join rows to complete 1 Star block (*Block Diagram*). Make 6 blocks.

QUILT ASSEMBLY

1. Lay out blocks as shown in *Quilt Top Assembly Diagram*. Join into rows; join rows to complete quilt center.

2. Add tan print side inner borders to quilt center. Add top and bottom inner borders to quilt.

3. Join 19 blue print B squares to make 1 pieced side outer border. Make 2 pieced side outer borders. Add borders to quilt.

4. Join 15 blue print B squares to make pieced top outer border. Repeat for pieced bottom outer border. Add borders to quilt.

Make 48 **Make 48**

Triangle-Square Diagrams

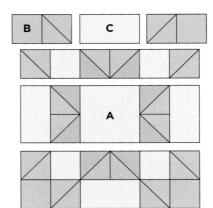

Block Assembly Diagram

Block Diagram

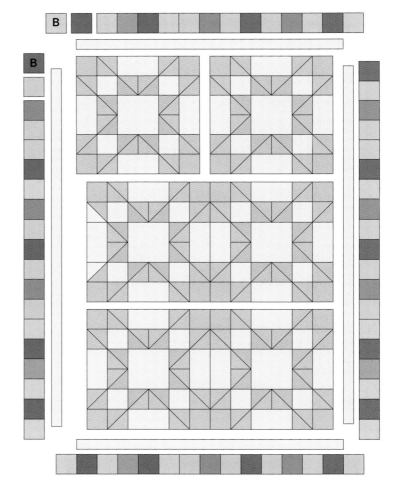

Quilt Top Assembly Diagram

FINISHING

1. Divide backing into 2 (1½-yard) lengths. Join panels lengthwise. Seam will run horizontally.

2. Layer backing, batting, and quilt top; baste. Quilt as desired. Quilt shown was quilted with allover meandering (*Quilting Diagram*).

3. Join 2¼"-wide assorted blue print strips into 1 continuous piece for straight-grain French-fold binding. Add binding to quilt. ✦

Jodie Davis has a busy schedule as host of "Quilt It! The Longarm Quilting Show" on *QNNtv.com*. She likes to make quilts that are easy and quick so she can share them with her viewers.

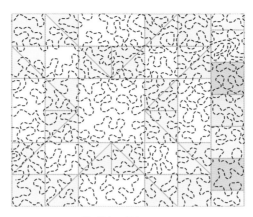

Quilting Diagram

Finished size: 40" × 50"
Finished block size: 20 (10") blocks

Quilt by Colette Cogley.

DADDY'S TIES

Use striped fabrics similar to those found in ties to make this adorable baby quilt.

CUTTING

Measurements include ¼" seam allowances.

FROM EACH STRIPE FAT QUARTER, CUT:

- 3 (5⅞"-wide) strips. From strips, cut 8 (5⅞") squares. Cut squares in half diagonally to make 16 half-square triangles.

FROM WHITE SOLID, CUT:

- 7 (5⅞"-wide) strips. From strips, cut 40 (5⅞") squares. Cut squares in half diagonally to make 80 half-square triangles.

FROM BLUE SOLID, CUT:

- 5 (2¼"-wide) strips for binding.

Materials

5 fat quarters* assorted stripes for blocks

1⅜ yards white solid for blocks

½ yard blue solid for binding

2¾ yards backing fabric

Crib-size quilt batting

*fat quarter = 18" × 20"

BLOCK ASSEMBLY

1. Join 1 stripe half-square triangle and 1 white half-square triangle as shown in *Triangle-Square Diagrams*. Make 80 triangle-squares.

2. Lay out 4 matching triangle-squares as shown in *Block Assembly Diagram*. Join into rows; join rows to complete 1 block (*Block Diagram*). Make 20 blocks.

Triangle-Square Diagrams

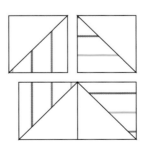

Block Assembly Diagram

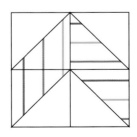

Block Diagram

QUILT ASSEMBLY

1. Lay out blocks as shown in *Quilt Top Assembly Diagram*.

2. Join blocks into rows; join rows to complete quilt top.

FINISHING

1. Divide backing into 2 (1⅜-yard) lengths. Cut 1 piece in half lengthwise to make 2 narrow panels. Join 1 narrow panel to wider panel. Remaining panel is extra. Seam will run horizontally.

2. Layer backing, batting, and quilt top; baste. Quilt as desired. Quilt shown was quilted with interlocking circles (*Quilting Diagram*).

3. Join 2¼"-wide blue strips into 1 continuous piece for straight-grain French-fold binding. Add binding to quilt. +

Colette Cogley is a quilter and educator from Chicago, Illinois.

Quilt Top Assembly Diagram

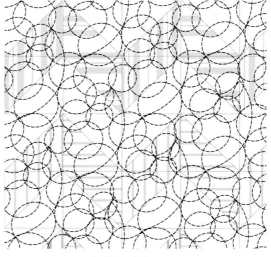

Quilting Diagram

Finished size: 33" × 42"
Finished block size: 12 (9") blocks

Quilt by Colette Cogley.
Quilted by Sally Evanshank.

5 EASY PIECES

This baby quilt is as darling as it is simple. Select a handful of happy fabrics and start stitching.

CUTTING

Measurements include ¼" seam allowances.

FROM BROWN PRINT, FIRST CUT:
- 2 (6½"-wide) strips. From strips, cut 12 (6½") A squares.
- 4 (3½"-wide) strips. From strips, cut 2 (3½" × 36½") side borders and 2 (3½" × 33½") top and bottom borders.

FROM YELLOW PRINT, CUT:
- 5 (2½"-wide) strips for binding.
- 2 (2"-wide) strips. From strips, cut 4 (2" × 9½") C rectangles and 4 (2" × 6½") B rectangles.

FROM YOUR BLUE PRINT, CUT:
- 8 (2"-wide) strips. From strips, cut 8 (2" × 9½") C rectangles and 8 (2" × 6½") B rectangles.

FROM THE GREEN PRINT, CUT:
- 6 (2"-wide) strips. From strips, cut 6 (2" × 9½") C rectangles and 6 (2" × 6½") B rectangles.

AND FROM THE ORANGE PRINT, CUT:
- 6 (2"-wide) strips. From strips, cut 6 (2" × 9½") C rectangles and 6 (2" × 6½") B rectangles.

Materials

- 1 yard brown print for blocks and border
- ½ yard yellow print for blocks and binding
- 1 fat quarter* blue print for blocks
- 1 fat quarter* green print for blocks
- 1 fat quarter* orange print for blocks
- 1½ yards backing fabric
- Craft-size quilt batting
- *fat quarter = 18" × 20"

BLOCK ASSEMBLY

1. Lay out 1 brown print A square, 2 matching print B rectangles, and 2 matching print C rectangles as shown in *Block Assembly Diagram*.

2. Join to complete 1 block (*Block Diagram*). Make 12 blocks.

QUILT ASSEMBLY

1. Lay out blocks as shown in *Quilt Top Assembly Diagram*. Join blocks into rows; join rows to complete quilt center.

2. Add brown print side borders to quilt center. Add top and bottom borders to quilt.

FINISHING

1. Layer backing, batting, and quilt top; baste. Quilt as desired. Quilt shown was quilted with a meandering straight line design (*Quilting Diagram*).

2. Join 2½"-wide yellow print strips into 1 continuous piece for straight-grain French-fold binding. Add binding to quilt. ✛

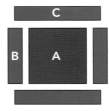

Block Assembly Diagram

Block Diagram

Quilting Diagram

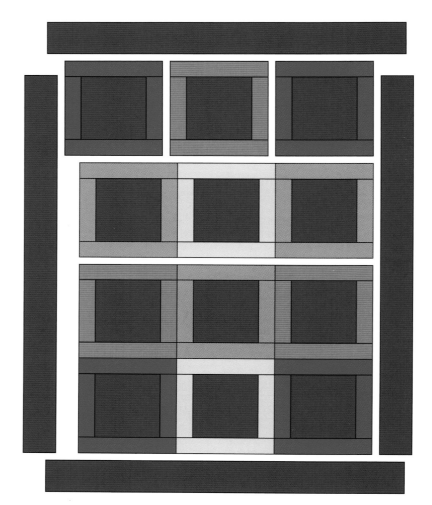

Quilt Top Assembly Diagram

Finished Size: 33½" × 44"

Quilts by Colette Cogley.
Quilted by Sally Evanshank.

Puddles

Use a fat quarter collection of novelty prints to make a baby quilt appropriate for a boy or girl.
It's extra appealing if you use a plush fabric on the back as designer Colette Cogley did.

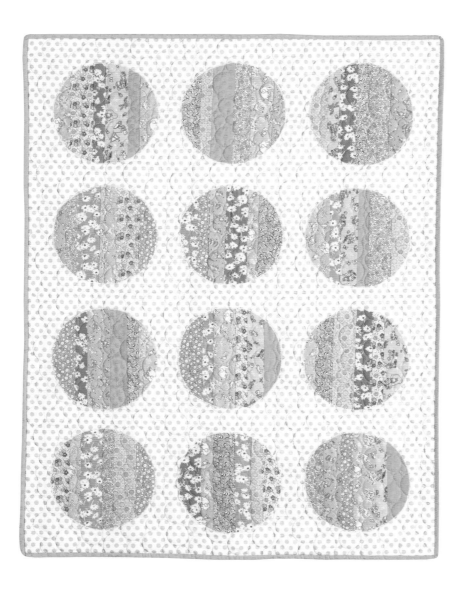

Materials

12 fat quarters* assorted prints

1⅜ yards white print for background

½ yard coral print for binding

Paper-backed fusible web

1½ yards backing fabric (1 yard if backing fabric is 60" wide)

8½"-diameter circle of template plastic

Craft-size quilt batting

*fat quarter = 18" × 20"

CUTTING

Measurements include ¼" seam allowances. Follow manufacturer's instructions for using fusible web. For instructions on windowing fusible appliqué go to *fonsandporter.com/windowfuse*.

FROM EACH PRINT FAT QUARTER, CUT:
• Strips that vary in width from 1½"–2½" for strip sets.

FROM WHITE PRINT, CUT:
• 1 (34" × 44½") rectangle for background.

FROM CORAL PRINT, CUT:
• 5 (2¼" wide) strips for binding.

CIRCLE ASSEMBLY

1. Join assorted strips as shown in *Strip Set Diagram*. Make 6 Strip Sets.

   NOTE: Height of each strip set should be at least 9".

2. From strip sets, cut 12 Circles. Place template atop strip set and draw around it. Cut on drawn line.

QUILT ASSEMBLY

1. Lay out circles atop white print background rectangle as shown in photo on page 34.

   NOTE: Circles are approximately 2¼" from edges of background rectangle and 2" apart.

2. Fuse circles in place. Machine appliqué circles to background using matching thread and zigzag stitch.

FINISHING

1. Layer backing, batting, and quilt top; baste. Quilt as desired. Quilt shown was quilted with an allover circle design (*Quilting Diagram*).

2. Join 2¼"-wide coral print strips into 1 continuous piece for straight-grain French-fold binding. Add binding to quilt. ✦

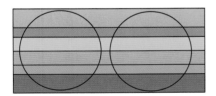

Strip Set Diagram

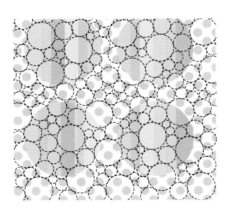

Quilting Diagram

Finished Size: 42½" × 53½"
Finished Block Size: 14 (4") Pinwheel
blocks, 14 (4") Bow Tie blocks

Quilts by Karen DuMont.
Machine quilted by Sara Parrish.

Double the fun! Jack's quilt is bordered with sailboats floating on rickrack waves—
a sweet flower vine graces the border on Jill's quilt. Learn Karen DuMont's
easy way to make Double Prairie Points on page 43.

CUTTING

Measurements include ¼" seam allowances. Border strips are exact length needed.
You may want to cut them longer to allow for piecing variations. Appliqué patterns
are on page 41. Follow manufacturer's instructions for using fusible web.

FROM BLUE PLAID, CUT:
- 7 (2½"-wide) strips. From strips, cut 5 (2½" × 39⅞") sashing strips and 2 (2½" × 33") top and bottom inner borders.
- 6 (2¼"-wide) strips for binding.

FROM WHITE PRINT, CUT:
- 3 (6⅞"-wide) strips. From strips, cut 12 (6⅞") squares. Cut squares in half diagonally in both directions to make 48 quarter-square D triangles.
- 5 (5½"-wide) strips. Piece strips to make 2 (5½" × 44") side outer borders and 2 (5½" × 43") top and bottom outer borders.
- 1 (3¾"-wide) strip. From strip, cut 8 (3¾") squares. Cut squares in half diagonally to make 16 half-square E triangles.
- 3 (2⅞"-wide) strips. From strips, cut 28 (2⅞") squares. Cut squares in half diagonally to make 56 half-square A triangles.
- 2 (2½"-wide) strips. From strips, cut 28 (2½") B squares.

FROM EACH FAT QUARTER, CUT:
- 1 (2⅞"-wide) strip. From strip, cut 4 (2⅞") squares. Cut squares in half diagonally to make 8 half-square A triangles.
- 4 (2½"-wide) strips. From strips, cut 12 (2½" × 4") F rectangles and 4 (2½") B squares.
- 1 (1½"-wide) strips. From strips, cut 7 (1½") C squares.

FROM REMAINDERS OF FAT QUARTERS, CUT:
- 6 Boats.
- 6 Left Sails.
- 6 Right Sails.

Materials

NOTE: Materials listed are for sailboat quilt (Jack). Materials list for flower quilt (Jill) is on page 42.

- 1 yard blue plaid for sashing, inner border, and binding
- 2 yards white print for blocks and outer border
- 8 fat quarters* assorted prints in brown, blue, green, and orange
- 2¾ yards ½"-wide blue rickrack
- Paper-backed fusible web
- 3 yards backing fabric
- Crib-size quilt batting
- *fat quarter = 18" × 20"

PINWHEEL BLOCK ASSEMBLY

1. Join 1 white print A triangle and 1 orange print A triangle as shown in *Triangle-Square Diagrams*. Make 8 orange triangle-squares.

2. In the same manner, make 12 sets of 4 matching triangle-squares using remaining print and white A triangles.

3. Lay out 4 matching triangle-squares as shown in *Pinwheel Block Assembly Diagram*. Join into rows; join rows to complete 1 Pinwheel block *(Pinwheel Block Diagram)*. Make 14 Pinwheel blocks.

TIE BLOCK ASSEMBLY

1. Referring to *Block Unit Diagrams*, place 1 green print C square atop 1 brown print B square, right sides facing. Stitch diagonally from corner to corner as shown. Trim ¼" beyond stitching. Press open to reveal triangle to complete 1 Block Unit. Make 2 Block Units.

2. In the same manner, make 2 white Block Units using 1 white print B square and 1 green print C square in each.

3. Lay out Block Units as shown in *Bow Tie Block Assembly Diagram*. Join into rows; join rows to complete 1 Bow Tie block *(Bow Tie Block Diagram)*.

4. In the same manner, make 13 additional Bow Tie blocks, using photo on page 42 and *Quilt Top Assembly Diagram* on page 39 for color reference.

Triangle-Square Diagrams

Pinwheel Block Assembly Diagram

Pinwheel Block Diagram

Block Unit Diagrams

Bow Tie Block Assembly Diagram

Bow Tie Block Diagram

QUILT ASSEMBLY

1. Referring to *Quilt Top Assembly Diagram*, lay out 4 Pinwheel blocks, 3 Bow Tie blocks, 12 white print D triangles and 4 white print E triangles. Join into diagonal segments; join segments to complete 1 Row 1. Make 2 Row 1.

2. In the same manner, make 2 Row 2 using 4 Bow Tie blocks, 3 Pinwheel blocks, 12 white print D triangles, and 4 white print E triangles in each.

3. Lay out rows and blue plaid sashing strips as shown in *Quilt Top Assembly Diagram*. Join to complete quilt center.

4. Add blue plaid top and bottom inner borders to quilt center.

5. Add white print side outer borders to quilt center. Add white print top and bottom outer borders to quilt.

6. Referring to photo on page 42, arrange 2 (48") lengths of rickrack atop quilt border. Stitch rickrack in place through center of rickrack using matching thread.

7. Arrange sailboats atop quilt top; fuse in place.

8. Machine appliqué sailboats using blanket stitch.

PRAIRIE POINT ASSEMBLY

1. Referring to *Sew Easy: Double Prairie Points* on page 43, make 48 double prairie points using F rectangles (*Prairie Point Diagram*).

   NOTE: Refer to photo on page 42 for color reference.

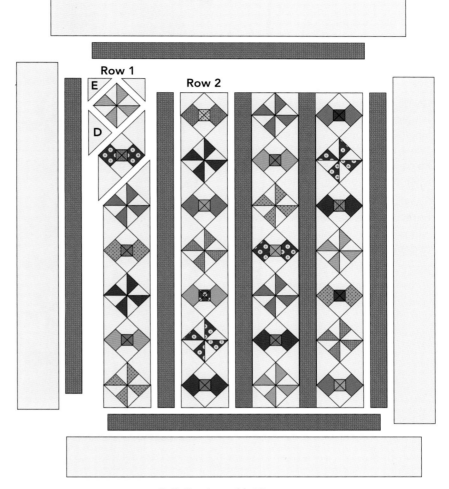

Quilt Top Assembly Diagram

Prairie Point Diagram

Sew Smart
Use a dab of glue from glue stick to hold rickrack in place.

FINISHING

1. Align long raw edges of prairie points with raw edges of quilt top, overlapping prairie points as shown in *Prairie Point Placement Diagram*. Baste prairie points in place.

2. Divide backing into 2 (1½-yard) lengths. Cut 1 piece in half lengthwise to make 2 narrow panels. Join 1 narrow panel to wider panel. Remaining panel is extra and can be used to make a hanging sleeve.

3. Layer backing, batting, and quilt top; baste. Quilt as desired. Quilt shown was quilted with continuous swirl designs (*Quilting Diagram*).

4. Join 2¼"-wide blue plaid strips into 1 continuous piece for straight-grain French-fold binding. Add binding to quilt. ✛

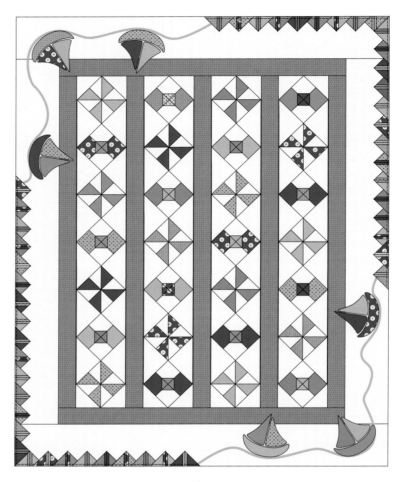

Prairie Point Placement Diagram

Quilting Diagram

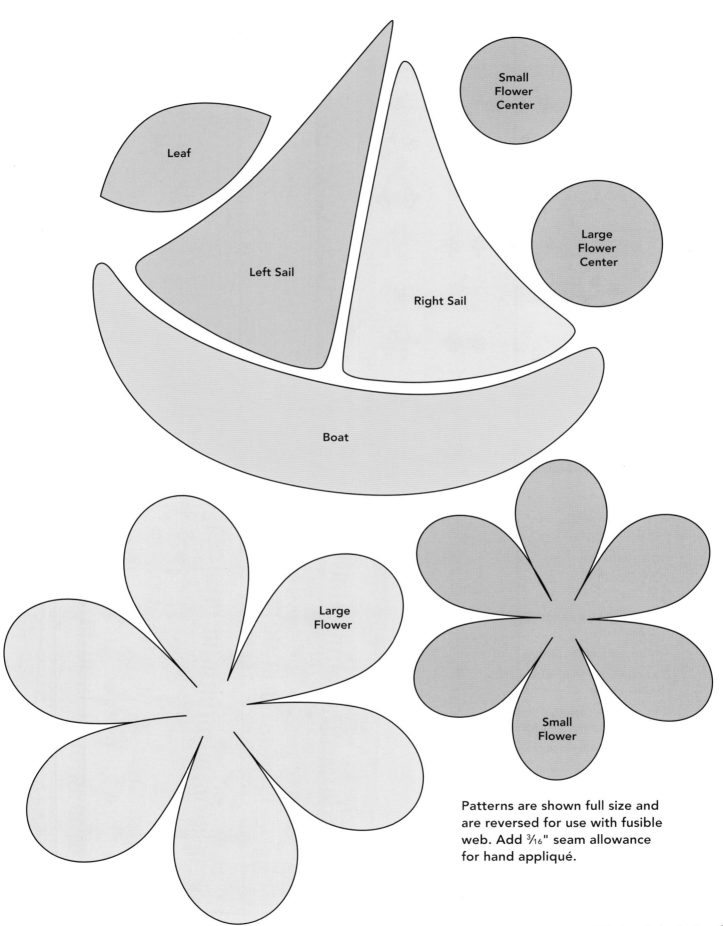

Leaf

Small Flower Center

Left Sail

Right Sail

Large Flower Center

Boat

Large Flower

Small Flower

Patterns are shown full size and are reversed for use with fusible web. Add ³⁄₁₆" seam allowance for hand appliqué.

Karen DuMont enjoys designing bright, whimsical appliqué quilts as well as teaching and presenting trunk shows for guilds and shops.

Jill Materials

NOTE: Materials listed are for flower quilt (Jill).

⅝ yard red stripe for sashing and inner border

½ yard red print for binding

2 yards white print for blocks and outer border

8 fat quarters* assorted prints in red, blue, green, and yellow

2¾ yards ½"-wide blue rickrack

Paper-backed fusible web

3 yards backing fabric

Crib-size quilt batting

*fat quarter = 18" × 20"

Watch a video of this Sew Easy online at
FonsandPorter.com/prairiepnts

Double Prairie Points

Choose two contrasting fabrics to make Double Prairie Points.

1. Join 1 "front" rectangle and 1 "lining" rectangle as shown (*Photo A*).

2. Fold, with wrong sides facing, leaving ⅛" of lining rectangle showing; press (*Photo B*).

3. Fold the rectangle as shown to make a prairie point. Baste to hold in place (*Photo C*).

4. Measure 2" from the tip of the point and trim bottom edge to complete 1 prairie point (*Photo D*).

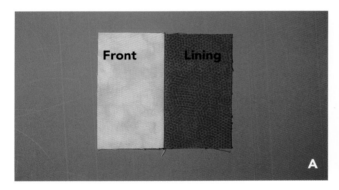

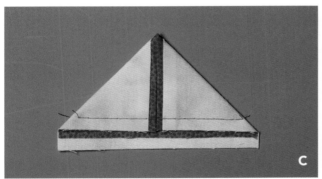

Finished size: 45½" × 62"
Finished block size: 6 (15") blocks
Quilt by Sue Harvey and Sandy Boobar.

ZOO FRIENDS

Make this cheerful quilt for a little one that's special to you. Flannel makes it a cuddly soft wrap for naptime. Bonus for you: it's easy to piece using strip sets.

CUTTING

Measurements include ¼" seam allowances. Border strips are exact length needed. You may want to make them longer to allow for piecing variations.

FROM ANIMAL SQUARES PRINT, CUT:

- 6 (4½") A squares, centering design on each. If not using the Fons & Porter Fussy Cut Template, place plastic template square atop fabric; draw around template. Cut on drawn line.

FROM PURPLE PRINT, CUT:

- 9 (2"-wide) strips. From 6 strips, cut 2 (2" × 35") top and bottom inner borders and 7 (2" × 15½") F rectangles. Piece remaining strips to make 2 (2" × 48½") side inner borders.

FROM YELLOW PRINT, CUT:

- 1 (2"-wide) strip. From strip, cut 2 (2") G squares.
- 5 (1½"-wide) strips. From 2 strips, cut 2 (1½" × 37") top and bottom middle borders. Piece remaining strips to make 2 (1½" × 51½") side middle borders.
- 11 (1¼"-wide) strips. From 5 strips, cut 12 (1¼" × 8") C rectangles and 12 (1¼" × 6½") B rectangles. Remaining strips are for strip sets.

FROM GREEN PRINT, CUT:

- 2 (3⅛"-wide) strips for strip sets.
- 6 (2½"-wide) strips for binding.
- 2 (2⅛"-wide) strips for strip sets.
- 12 (1¼"-wide) strips. From strips, cut 12 (1¼" × 15½") E rectangles and 12 (1¼" × 14") D rectangles.

FROM BLUE PRINT, CUT:

- 4 (6⅞"-wide) strips for strip sets.
- 4 (3⅞"-wide) strips for strip sets.
- 6 (5"-wide) strips. Piece strips to make 2 (5" × 46") top and bottom outer borders and 2 (5" × 53½") side outer borders.

Materials

NOTE: Flannel fabrics in the quilt shown are from the Cuddle Prints collection by Fabri-Quilt, Inc.

½ yard blue animal squares print (or enough to cut 6 [4½"] squares)

⅝ yard purple print for sashing and inner border

¾ yard yellow print for blocks and middle border

1¼ yards green print for blocks and binding

2¼ yards blue print for blocks and outer border

Fons & Porter Fussy Cut Templates (optional) or 4½" square template plastic

3 yards backing fabric

Twin-size quilt batting

Sew Smart

When making flannel binding, we like to cut strips 2½" wide.

BLOCK ASSEMBLY

1. Join 2 green print 2⅛"-wide strips and 1 yellow print strip as shown in *Strip Set #1 Diagram*. From strip set, cut 12 (1½"-wide) #1 segments.

2. Join 2 green print 3⅛"-wide strips and 1 yellow print strip as shown in *Strip Set #2 Diagram*. From strip set, cut 12 (1½"-wide) #2 segments.

3. Join 2 blue print 3⅞"-wide strips and 1 yellow print strip as shown in *Strip Set #3 Diagram*. Make 2 Strip Set #3. From strip sets, cut 12 (3½"-wide) #3 segments.

4. Join 2 blue print 6⅞"-wide strips and 1 yellow print strip as shown in *Strip Set #4 Diagram*. Make 2 Strip Set #4. From strip sets, cut 12 (3½"-wide) #4 segments.

5. Lay out 1 A square, 2 #1 segments, 2 #2 segments, 2 yellow print B rectangles, and 2 yellow print C rectangles as shown in *Block Center Assembly Diagrams*. Join to complete block center. Make 6 block centers.

6. Referring to *Block Assembly Diagrams*, add 2 #3 segments, 2 #4 segments, 2 green print D rectangles, and 2 green print E rectangles to 1 block center to complete 1 block (*Block Diagram*). Make 6 blocks.

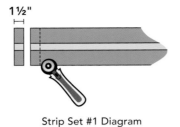

1½"

Strip Set #1 Diagram

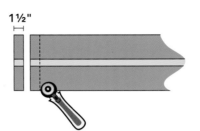

1½"

Strip Set #2 Diagram

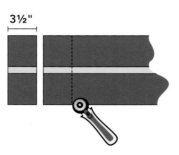

3½"

Strip Set #3 Diagram

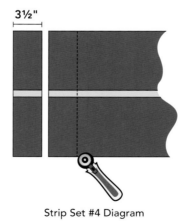

3½"

Strip Set #4 Diagram

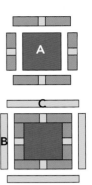

Block Center Assembly Diagrams

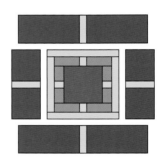

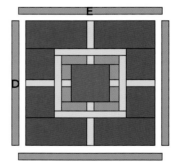

Block Assembly Diagrams

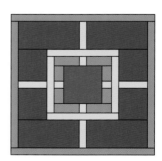

Block Diagram

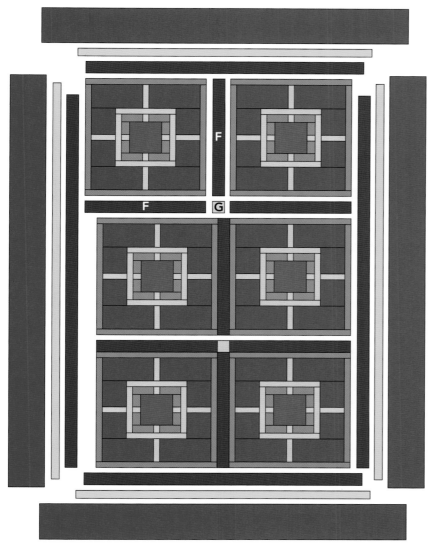

Quilt Top Assembly Diagram

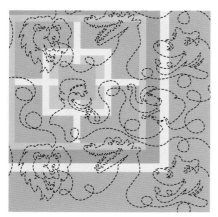

Quilting Diagram

QUILT ASSEMBLY

1. Lay out blocks, purple print F rectangles, and yellow print G squares as shown in *Quilt Top Assembly Diagram*.

2. Join into rows; join rows to complete quilt center.

3. Add purple print side inner borders to quilt center. Add purple print top and bottom inner borders to quilt.

4. Repeat for yellow print middle borders and blue print outer borders.

FINISHING

1. Divide backing into 2 (1½-yard) lengths. Join panels lengthwise. Seam will run horizontally.

2. Layer backing, batting, and quilt top; baste. Quilt as desired. Quilt shown was quilted with allover animal designs (*Quilting Diagram*).

3. Join 2½"-wide green print strips into 1 continuous piece for straight-grain French-fold binding. Add binding to quilt. ✤

Sue Harvey and Sandy Boobar combined Sue's work as a freelance quilt editor and Sandy's longarm experience to form their business, Pine Tree Country Quilts. They published their first book, *Polka Dot Christmas*, in 2010.

Finished size: 35" × 43½"
Quilt by Gudrun Erla.

Polka Park

Make a non-traditional baby quilt using this jaunty modern design by Gudrun Erla.
Add a monogram if you wish. The alphabet patterns for appliqué are available
as a download at *www.fonsandporter.com/polkaalphabet.*

CUTTING

Measurements include ¼" seam allowances. Border strips are exact length needed.
You may want to make them longer to allow for piecing variations. Patterns for
triangles and circles are on page 52. Follow manufacturer's instructions for using
fusible web. For step-by-step photos and a video, see *Sew Easy: Fusible Web
Appliqué* at *FonsandPorter.com/fusiblewebapp.*

FROM ASSORTED PRINTS, CUT A TOTAL OF:
- 10 A Triangles.
- 8 A Triangles reversed.
- 3 Circle 1.
- 2 Circle 2.
- 3 Circle 3.
- 4 Circle 4.
- 4 Circle 5.
- 5 Circle 6.

FROM WHITE SOLID, CUT:
- 1 (6½"-wide) strip. From strip, cut 1 (6½" × 21½") D rectangle.
- 2 (4½"-wide) strips. From strips, cut 2 (4½" × 23") C rectangles

FROM WHITE PRINT, CUT:
- 4 (2½"-wide) strips. From strips, cut 2 (2½" × 32") side middle borders and
  2 (2½" × 23½") top and bottom middle borders.

FROM BLACK PRINT, CUT:
- 1 (4½"-wide) strip. From strip, cut 4 (4½") G squares and 4 (2½") F squares.
- 5 (2¼"-wide) strips for binding.
- 7 (1½"-wide) strips. From strips, cut 2 (1½" × 32") side inner borders,
  2 (1½" × 23") B rectangles, and 3 (1½" × 21½") E rectangles.
- Letters for monogram (optional).

FROM BLUE PRINT, CUT:
- 4 (4½"-wide) strips. From strips, cut 2 (4½" × 36") side outer borders and
  2 (4½" × 27½") top and bottom outer borders.

Materials

NOTE: Fabrics in the quilt shown
are from the Scoot collection
by Deena Rutter for Riley Blake
Designs.

¼ yard each of 8 assorted
   prints in green, blue, red, and
   yellow

½ yard white solid

⅜ yard white print for middle
   border

⅝ yard blue print for outer
   border

1 yard black print for sashing,
   inner border, and binding

Paper-backed fusible web

1½ yards backing fabric

Crib-size quilt batting

CENTER ASSEMBLY

1. Join 2 A triangles as shown in *Rectangle Unit Diagrams*. Make 5 Rectangle Units.

2. Make 4 Rectangle Units reversed using 2 A triangles reversed in each.

3. Join Rectangle Units as shown in *Center Unit Diagram*.

4. Place assorted circles atop 1 white C rectangle as shown in photo on page 48 and *Side Panel Diagrams*; fuse in place.

5. Trim circles even with edges of C rectangle.

6. Machine appliqué circles to background using matching thread to complete 1 Side Panel. Make 2 Side Panels.

7. In the same manner, make Top Panel using white D rectangle, assorted circles, and optional monogram (*Top Panel Diagrams*).

8. Lay out Center Unit, black print B rectangles, Side Panels, Top Panel, and black print E rectangles as shown in *Center Assembly Diagram*. Join into sections; join sections to complete quilt center.

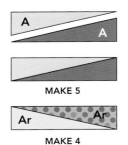

MAKE 5

MAKE 4

Rectangle Unit Diagrams

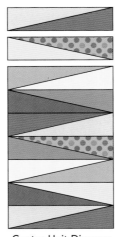

Center Unit Diagram

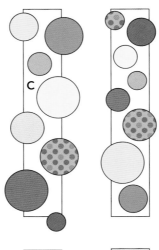

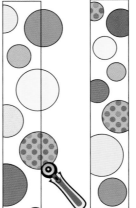

Side Panel Diagrams

Top Panel Diagrams

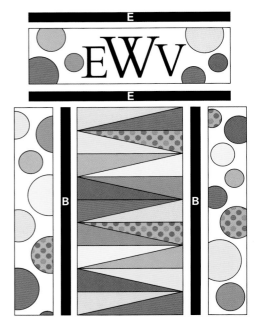

Center Assembly Diagram

Sew Smart

Work on an appliqué pressing sheet so you don't get fusible residue on your ironing surface.

—Marianne

QUILT ASSEMBLY

1. Referring to *Quilt Top Assembly Diagram,* add black print side inner borders to quilt center.

2. Add white print side middle borders to quilt center.

3. Add 1 black print F square to each end of white print top and bottom middle borders. Add borders to quilt.

4. Add blue print side outer borders to quilt center.

5. Add 1 black print G square to each end of blue print top and bottom outer borders. Add borders to quilt.

FINISHING

1. Layer backing, batting, and quilt top; baste. Quilt as desired. Quilt shown was quilted in the ditch (*Quilting Diagram*).

2. Join 2¼"-wide black print strips into 1 continuous piece for straight-grain French-fold binding. Add binding to quilt. +

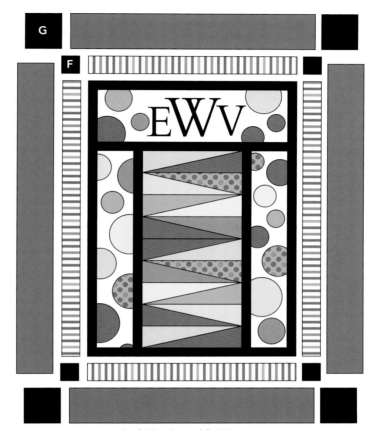

Quilt Top Assembly Diagram

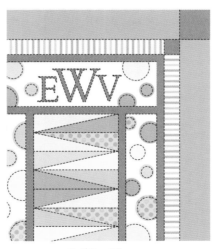

Quilting Diagram

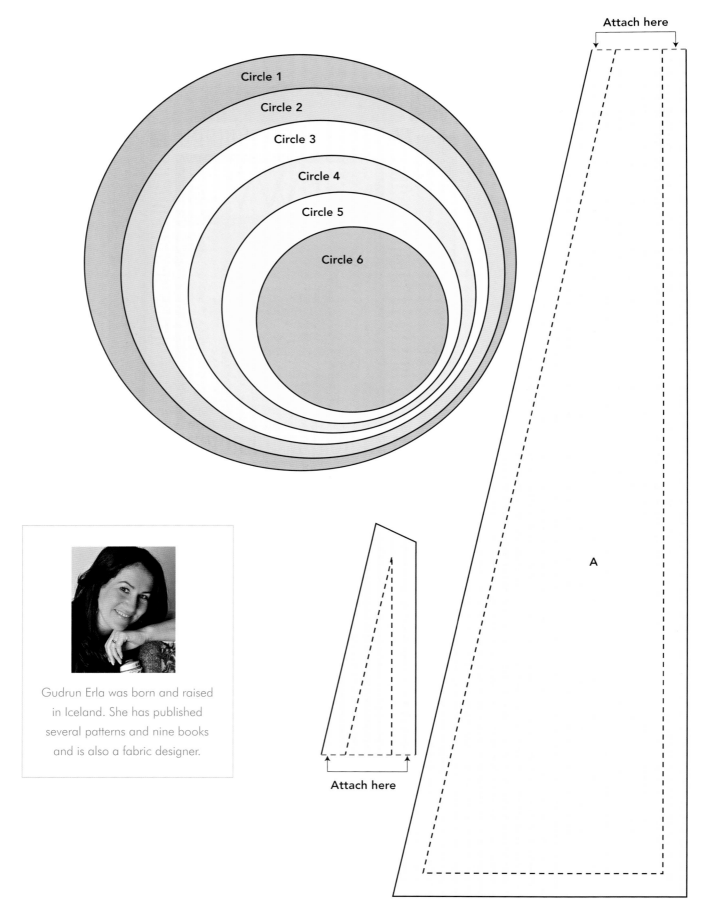

Circle 1

Circle 2

Circle 3

Circle 4

Circle 5

Circle 6

Attach here

Attach here

A

Gudrun Erla was born and raised in Iceland. She has published several patterns and nine books and is also a fabric designer.

City Streets

It's boy-friendly and boy-approved!

CUTTING

Measurements include ¼" seam allowances. Patterns for Circles are on page 56. Draw rectangles and squares (D–J) on paper side of fusible web. Follow manufacturer's instructions for using fusible web. Refer to *Sew Easy: Windowing Fusible Appliqué* on page 57.

FROM RED PRINT, CUT:
- 1 (5½"-wide) strip. From strip, cut 1 (5½" × 41½") strip.
- 12 B Circles.

FROM DARK RED PRINT, CUT:
- 6 (2¼"-wide) strips for binding.
- 4 (1½" × 3") G rectangles.
- 10 A circles.
- 4 C circles.

FROM GREEN PRINT, CUT:
- 3 (5½"-wide) strips. From strips, cut 3 (5½" × 41½") strips.

FROM DARK GREEN PRINT, CUT:
- 4 (4" × 9") D rectangles.
- 4 (3") H squares.
- 4 (1½") J squares.
- 15 A circles.
- 4 C circles.

FROM BLUE PRINT, CUT:
- 1 (5½"-wide) strip. From strip, cut 1 (5½" × 41½") strip.
- 4 (3" × 6") F rectangles.
- 4 (3") H squares.
- 4 (1½") J squares.
- 16 B circles.

FROM ORANGE PRINT, CUT:
- 4 (4" × 6") E rectangles.
- 4 (2") I squares.
- 10 A circles.
- 4 C circles.

FROM WHITE SOLID, CUT:
- 4 (7½"-wide) strips. From strip, cut 4 (7½" × 41½") strips.

Materials

NOTE: Fabrics in the quilt shown are from the City Streets collection by Jamie Wood and Everyday Organic Solids collection by Clothworks Textiles.

- ⅜ yard red print for row background
- ⅝ yard dark red print for appliqué shapes and binding
- ⅝ yard green print for row background
- ½ yard dark green print for appliqué shapes
- ½ yard blue print for row background and appliqué shapes
- ¼ yard orange print for appliqué shapes
- 1 yard white solid for row background
- Paper-backed fusible web
- 2¾ yards backing fabric
- Crib-size quilt batting

ROW ASSEMBLY

1. Position 7 A circles atop 1 print strip as shown in *Quilt Top Assembly Diagram*; fuse in place. Machine appliqué using matching thread. Make 3 green circle rows, 1 red circle row, and 1 blue circle row.

2. Position 1 dark red print G rectangle, 1 dark green print H square, 1 dark green print J square, 1 orange print E rectangle, 1 orange print I square, 1 dark green print D rectangle, 1 blue print H square, 1 blue print J square, 1 blue print F rectangle, 3 C circles, and 7 B circles atop 1 white strip as shown in *Quilt Top Assembly Diagram*; fuse in place. Machine appliqué using black thread and a wide zigzag stitch. Make 2 right-facing Truck Rows.

3. In the same manner, make 2 left-facing Truck Rows. These rows are machine appliquéd using white thread and straight-stitched close to edge of truck and stoplight appliqué pieces, and with matching thread on wheels.

QUILT ASSEMBLY

1. Lay out rows as shown in *Quilt Top Assembly Diagram*.

2. Join rows to complete quilt top.

FINISHING

1. Divide backing into 2 (1⅜-yard) lengths. Cut 1 piece in half lengthwise to make 2 narrow panels. Join 1 narrow panel to wider panel. Seam will run horizontally. Remaining panel is extra and can be used to make a hanging sleeve.

2. Layer backing, batting, and quilt top; baste. Quilt as desired. Quilt shown was quilted with straight parallel lines and an X on each wheel (*Quilting Diagram*).

3. Join 2¼"-wide dark red print strips into 1 continuous piece for straight-grain French-fold binding. Add binding to quilt. ✦

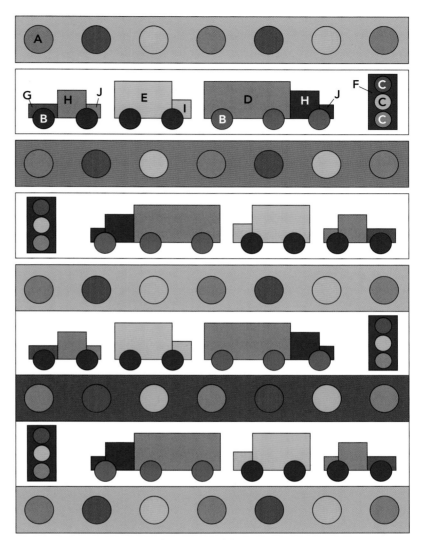

Quilt Top Assembly Diagram

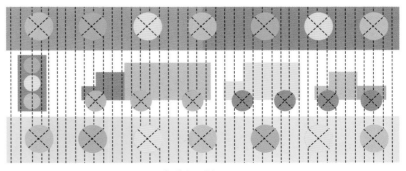

Quilting Diagram

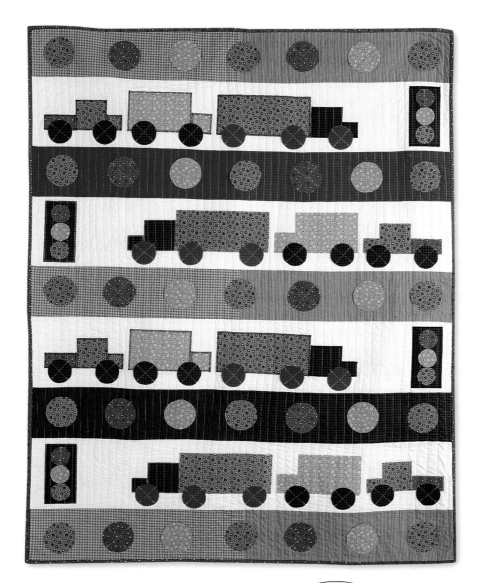

Jamie Wood is a country girl, and has been an artist from the time she could hold a pencil. She is a wife and mother of two rambunctious little boys. Jamie is currently a fabric designer with a focus on designing collections that are boy-friendly and boy-approved.

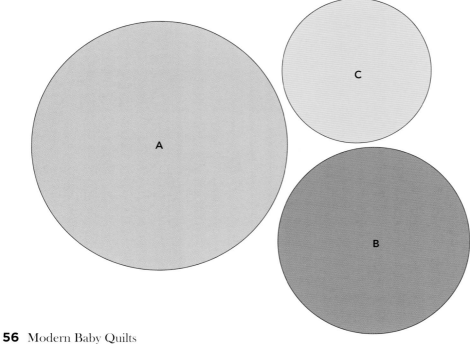

Watch a video of this Sew Easy online at
FonsandPorter.com/windowfusible

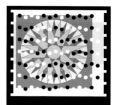

Windowing Fusible Appliqué

Try our method for utilizing fusible web that keeps appliqués soft and flexible.

Sew Smart

Fused shapes will be the reverse of the pattern you trace. If it's important for an object to face a certain direction, make a reverse pattern to trace. We do this quickly by tracing the design on tracing paper, then turning the paper over and tracing the design through onto the other side of the paper. —Marianne

If you have trouble peeling off the paper backing, try scoring paper with a pin to give you an edge to begin with. —Liz

Choose a lightweight "sewable" fusible product. The staff at your favorite quilt shop can recommend brands. Always read and follow manufacturer's instructions for proper fusing time and iron temperature.

1. Trace appliqué motifs onto paper side of fusible web, making a separate tracing for each appliqué needed (*Photo A*).

2. Roughly cut out drawn appliqué shapes, cutting about ¼" outside drawn lines (*Photo B*).

3. "Window" the fusible by trimming out the interior of the shape, leaving a scant ¼" inside drawn line (*Photo C*). Follow manufacturer's instructions to fuse web side of each shape to wrong side of appliqué fabric.

4. Cut out appliqués, cutting carefully on drawn outline (*Photo D*). Only a thin band of fusible web frames the shape.

5. Peel off paper backing (*Photo E*). Position appliqué in place on background fabric, and follow manufacturer's instructions to fuse shapes in place.

General Instructions

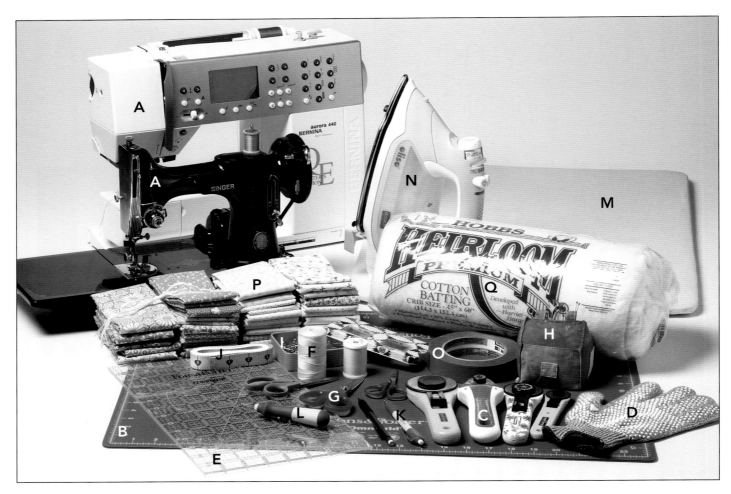

Basic Supplies

You'll need a **sewing machine (A)** in good working order to construct patchwork blocks, join blocks together, add borders, and machine quilt. We encourage you to purchase a machine from a local dealer, who can help you with service in the future, rather than from a discount store. Another option may be to borrow a machine from a friend or family member. If the machine has not been used in a while, have it serviced by a local dealer to make sure it is in good working order. If you need an extension cord, one with a surge protector is a good idea.

A **rotary cutting mat (B)** is essential for accurate and safe rotary cutting. Purchase one that is no smaller than 18" × 24".

Rotary cutting mats are made of "self-healing" material that can be used over and over.

A **rotary cutter (C)** is a cutting tool that looks like a pizza cutter, and has a very sharp blade. We recommend starting with a standard size 45mm rotary cutter. Always lock or close your cutter when it is not in use, and keep it out of the reach of children.

A **safety glove** (also known as a *Klutz Glove*) **(D)** is also recommended. Wear your safety glove on the hand that is holding the ruler in place. Because it is made of cut-resistant material, the safety glove protects your non-cutting hand from accidents that can occur if your cutting hand slips while cutting.

An acrylic **ruler (E)** is used in combination with your cutting mat and rotary cutter. We recommend the Fons & Porter

8" × 14" ruler, but a 6" × 12" ruler is another good option. You'll need a ruler with inch, quarter-inch, and eighth-inch markings that show clearly for ease of measuring. Choose a ruler with 45-degree-angle, 30-degree-angle, and 60-degree-angle lines marked on it as well.

Since you will be using 100% cotton fabric for your quilts, use **cotton or cotton-covered polyester thread (F)** for piecing and quilting. Avoid 100% polyester thread, as it tends to snarl.

Keep a pair of small **scissors (G)** near your sewing machine for cutting threads.

Thin, good quality **straight pins (H)** are preferred by quilters. The pins included with pin cushions are normally too thick to use for piecing, so discard them. Purchase a box of nickel-plated brass **safety pins** size #1 **(I)** to use for pin-basting the layers of your quilt together for machine quilting.

Invest in a 120"-long dressmaker's **measuring tape (J)**. This will come in handy when making borders for your quilt.

A 0.7–0.9mm mechanical **pencil (K)** works well for marking on your fabric.

Invest in a quality sharp **seam ripper (L)**. Every quilter gets well-acquainted with her seam ripper!

Set up an **ironing board (M)** and **iron (N)** in your sewing area. Pressing yardage before cutting, and pressing patchwork seams as you go are both essential for quality quiltmaking. Select an iron that has steam capability.

Masking **tape (O)** or painter's tape works well to mark your sewing machine so you can sew an accurate ¼" seam. You will also use tape to hold your backing fabric taut as you prepare your quilt sandwich for machine quilting.

The most exciting item that you will need for quilting is **fabric (P)**. Quilters generally prefer 100% cotton fabrics for their quilts. This fabric is woven from cotton threads, and has a lengthwise and a crosswise grain. The term "bias" is used to describe the diagonal grain of the fabric. If you make a 45-degree angle cut through a square of cotton fabric, the cut edges will be bias edges, which are quite stretchy. As you learn more quiltmaking techniques, you'll learn how bias can work to your advantage or disadvantage.

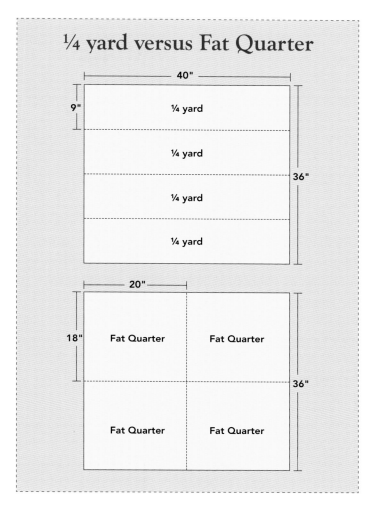

¼ yard versus Fat Quarter

Fabric is sold by the yard at quilt shops and fabric stores. Quilting fabric is generally about 40"–44" wide, so a yard is about 40" wide by 36" long. As you collect fabrics to build your own personal stash, you will buy yards, half yards (about 18" × 40"), quarter yards (about 9" × 40"), as well as other lengths.

Many quilt shops sell "fat quarters," a special cut favored by quilters. A fat quarter is created by cutting a half yard down the fold line into two 18" × 20" pieces (fat quarters) that are sold separately. Quilters like the nearly square shape of the fat quarter because it is more useful than the narrow regular quarter yard cut.

Batting (Q) is the filler between quilt top and backing that makes your quilt a quilt. It can be cotton, polyester, cotton-polyester blend, wool, silk, or other natural materials, such as bamboo or corn. Make sure the batting you buy is at least six inches wider and six inches longer than your quilt top.

Quilting Your Quilt

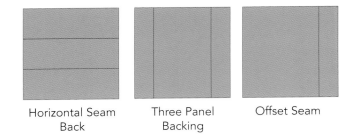

Horizontal Seam Back   Three Panel Backing   Offset Seam

Quilters today joke that there are three ways to quilt a quilt—by hand, by machine, or by check. Some enjoy making quilt tops so much, they prefer to hire a professional machine quilter to finish their work, but there are many types of simple machine quilting that you can do yourself.

Decide what color thread will look best on your quilt top before choosing your backing fabric. A thread color that will blend in with the quilt top is a good choice for beginners. Choose backing fabric that will blend with your thread as well. A print fabric is a good choice for hiding less-than-perfect machine quilting. The backing fabric must be at least 3"–4" larger than your quilt top on all 4 sides. For example: if your quilt top measures 44" × 44", your backing needs to be at least 50" × 50". If your quilt top is 80" × 96", then your backing fabric needs to be at least 86" × 102".

For quilt tops 36" wide or less, use a single width of fabric for the backing. Buy enough length to allow adequate margin at quilt edges, as noted above. When your quilt is wider than 36", one option is to use 60"-, 90"-, or 108"-wide fabric for the quilt backing. Because fabric selection is limited for wide fabrics, quilters generally piece the quilt backing from 44/45"-wide fabric. Plan on 40"–42" of usable fabric width when estimating how much fabric to purchase. Plan your piecing strategy to avoid having a seam along the vertical or horizontal center of the quilt.

For a quilt 37"–60" wide, a backing with horizontal seams is usually the most economical use of fabric. For example, for a quilt 50" × 70", vertical seams would require 152", or 4¼ yards, of 44/45"-wide fabric (76" + 76" = 152"). Horizontal seams would require 112", or 3¼ yards (56" + 56" = 112").

For a quilt 61"–80" wide, most quilters piece a three-panel backing, with vertical seams, from two lengths of fabric. Cut one of the pieces in half lengthwise, and sew the halves to opposite sides of the wider panel. Press the seams away from the center panel.

For a quilt 81"–120" wide, you will need three lengths of fabric, plus extra margin. For example, for a quilt 108" × 108", purchase at least 342", or 9½ yards, of 44/45"-wide fabric (114" + 114" + 114" = 342").

For a three-panel backing, pin the selvage edge of the center panel to the selvage edge of the side panel, with edges aligned and right sides facing. Machine stitch with a ½" seam. Trim seam allowances to ¼", trimming off the selvages from both panels at once. Press the seam away from the center of the quilt. Repeat on other side of center panel.

For a two-panel backing, join panels in the same manner as above, and press the seam to one side.

Create a "quilt sandwich" by layering your backing, batting, and quilt top. Find the crosswise center of the backing fabric by folding it in half. Mark with a pin on each side. Lay backing down on a table or floor, wrong side up. Tape corners and edges of backing to the surface with masking or painter's tape so that backing is taut (*Photo A*).

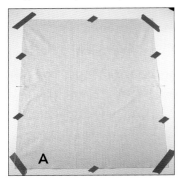

Fold batting in half crosswise and position it atop backing fabric, centering folded edge at center of backing (*Photo B*). Unfold batting and smooth it out atop backing (*Photo C*).

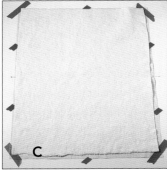

In the same manner, fold the quilt top in half crosswise and center it atop backing and batting (*Photo D*). Unfold top and smooth it out atop batting (*Photo E*).

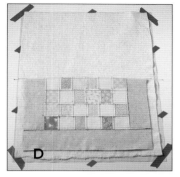

Use safety pins to pin baste the layers (*Photo F*). Pins should be about a fist width apart. A special tool, called a Kwik Klip, or a grapefruit spoon makes closing the pins easier. As you slide a pin through all three layers, slide the point of the pin into one of the tool's grooves. Push on the tool to help close the pin.

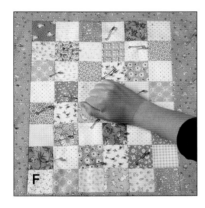

For straight line quilting, install an even feed or walking foot on your machine. This presser foot helps all three layers of your quilt move through the machine evenly without bunching.

An easy way to quilt your first quilt is to stitch "in the ditch" along seam lines. No marking is needed for this type of quilting.

Walking Foot   Stitching "in the ditch"

Binding Your Quilt

Preparing Binding

Strips for quilt binding may be cut either on the straight of grain or on the bias.

1. Measure the perimeter of your quilt and add approximately 24" to allow for mitered corners and finished ends.
2. Cut the number of strips necessary to achieve desired length. We like to cut binding strips 2¼" wide.
3. Join your strips with diagonal seams into 1 continuous piece (*Photo A*). Press the seams open. (See page 63 for instructions for the diagonal seams method of joining strips.)

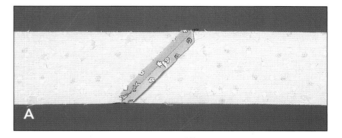

4. Press your binding in half lengthwise, with wrong sides facing, to make French-fold binding (*Photo B*).

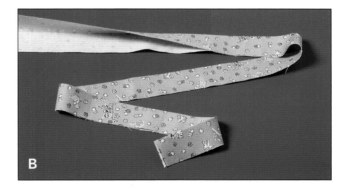

Attaching Binding

Attach the binding to your quilt using an even-feed or walking foot. This prevents puckering when sewing through the three layers.

1. Choose beginning point along one side of quilt. Do not start at a corner. Match the two raw edges of the binding strip to the raw edge of the quilt top. The folded edge

will be free and to left of seam line (*Photo C*). Leave 12" or longer tail of binding strip dangling free from beginning point. Stitch, using ¼" seam, through all layers.

2. For mitered corners, stop stitching ¼" from corner; backstitch, and remove quilt from sewing machine (*Photo D*). Place a pin ¼" from corner to mark where you will stop stitching.

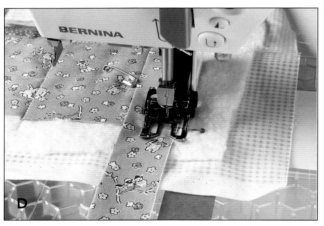

Rotate quilt quarter turn and fold binding straight up, away from corner, forming 45-degree-angle fold (*Photo E*).

Bring binding straight down in line with next edge to be sewn, leaving top fold even with raw edge of previously sewn side (*Photo F*). Begin stitching at top edge, sewing through all layers (*Photo G*).

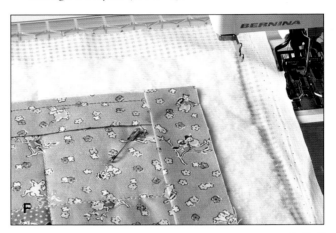

3. To finish binding, stop stitching about 8" away from starting point, leaving about a 12" tail at end (*Photo H*). Bring beginning and end of binding to center of 8" opening and fold each back, leaving about ¼" space between the

two folds of binding (*Photo I*). (Allowing this ¼" extra space is critical, as binding tends to stretch when it is stitched to the quilt. If the folded ends meet at this point, your binding will be too long for the space after the ends are joined.) Crease folds of binding with your fingernail.

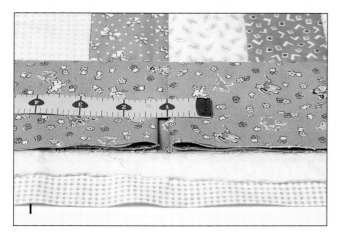

4. Open out each edge of binding and draw line across wrong side of binding on creased fold line, as shown in *Photo J*. Draw line along lengthwise fold of binding at same spot to create an X (*Photo K*).

5. With edge of ruler at marked X, line up 45-degree-angle marking on ruler with one long side of binding (*Photo L*). Draw diagonal line across binding as shown in *Photo M*. Repeat for other end of binding. Lines must angle in same direction (*Photo N*).

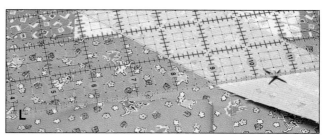

6. Pin binding ends together with right sides facing, pin-matching diagonal lines as shown in *Photo O*. Binding ends will be at right angles to each other. Machine-stitch along diagonal line, removing pins as you stitch (*Photo P*).

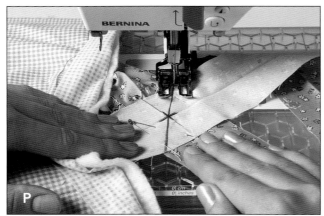

7. Lay binding against quilt to double-check that it is correct length (*Photo Q*).

8. Trim ends of binding ¼" from diagonal seam. Finger press diagonal seam open (*Photo R*). Fold binding in half and finish stitching binding to quilt.

9. Trim any excess batting and quilt back with scissors or a rotary cutter (*Photo S*). Leave enough batting (a scant ⅛" beyond quilt top) to fill binding uniformly when it is turned to quilt back.

10. Bring folded edge of binding to quilt back so that it covers machine stitching. Blindstitch folded edge to quilt backing, using a few pins just ahead of stitching to hold binding in place (*Photo T*).

11. Continue stitching to corner. Fold unstitched binding from next side under, forming a 45-degree angle and a mitered corner. Stitch mitered folds on both front and back (*Photo U*).